T

Spiritual Warfare

Disarming the Enemy Through the Power of God

A. SCOTT MOREAU

FISHERMAN
BIBLE STUDYGUIDES

SPIRITUAL WARFARE

All Scripture quotations are taken from the *Holy Bible, New International Version*®. *NIV*®. Copyright ©
1973, 1978, 1984 by International Bible Society. Used by permission of Zondervan Publishing House.
All rights reserved.

Trade Paperback ISBN 978-0-87788-777-5

Copyright © 1995, 2004 by A. Scott Moreau

Published in the United States by WaterBrook, an imprint of the Crown Publishing Group, a division of
Penguin Random House LLC, New York.

Printed in the United States of America
2017

25 24 23 22 21 20 19

Contents

How to Use This Studyguide

isherman studyguides are based on the inductive approach to Bible study. Inductive study is discovery study; we discover what the Bible says as we ask questions about its content and search for answers. This is quite different from the process in which a teacher *tells* a group *about* the Bible—what it means and what to do about it. In inductive study, God speaks directly to each of us through his Word.

A group functions best when a leader keeps the discussion on target, but the leader is neither the teacher nor the "answer person." A leader's responsibility is to *ask*—not *tell*. The answers come from the text itself as group members examine, discuss, and think together about the passage.

There are four kinds of questions in each study. The first is an *approach question*. Asked and answered before the Bible passage is read, this question breaks the ice and helps you start thinking about the topic of the Bible study. It begins to reveal where thoughts and feelings need to be transformed by Scripture.

Some of the earlier questions in each study are *observation questions*—who, what, where, when, and how—designed to help you learn some basic facts about the passage of Scripture.

Once you know what the Bible says, you need to ask, *What does it mean?* These *interpretation questions* help you discover the writer's basic message.

Next come *application questions*, which ask, *What does it mean to me?* They challenge you to live out the Scripture's life-transforming message.

Fisherman studyguides provide spaces between questions for jotting down responses as well as any related questions you would like to raise in the group. Each group member should have a copy of the studyguide and may take a turn in leading the group.

A group should use any accurate, modern translation of the Bible such as the *New International Version,* the *New American Standard Bible,* the *New Living Translation,* the *New Revised Standard Version,* the *New Jerusalem Bible,* or the *Good News Bible.* (Other translations or paraphrases of the Bible may be referred to when additional help is needed.) Bible commentaries should not be brought to a Bible study because they tend to dampen discussion and keep people from thinking for themselves.

SUGGESTIONS FOR GROUP LEADERS

1. Thoroughly read and study the Bible passage before the meeting. Get a firm grasp on its themes and begin applying its teachings for yourself. Pray that the Holy Spirit will "guide you into all truth" (John 16:13) so that your leadership will guide others.

2. If any of the studyguide's questions seem ambiguous or unnatural to you, rephrase them, feeling free to add others that seem necessary to bring out the meaning of a verse.

3. Begin (and end) the study promptly. Start by asking someone to pray that every participant will both understand the passage and be open to its transforming power. Remember, the Holy Spirit is the teacher, not you!

4. Ask for volunteers to read the passages aloud.

5. As you ask the studyguide's questions in sequence, encourage everyone to participate in the discussion. If some are silent, try gently suggesting, "Let's have an answer from someone who hasn't spoken up yet."

6. If a question comes up that you can't answer, don't be afraid to admit that you're baffled. Assign the topic as a research project for someone to report on next week, or say, "I'll do some studying and let you know what I find out."

7. Keep the discussion moving, but be sure it stays focused. Though a certain number of tangents are inevitable, you'll want to quickly bring the discussion back to the topic at hand. Also, learn to pace the discussion so that you finish the lesson in the time allotted.

8. Don't be afraid of silences; some questions take time to answer, and some people need time to gather courage to speak. If silence persists, rephrase your question, but resist the temptation to answer it yourself.

9. If someone comes up with an answer that is clearly illogical or unbiblical, ask for further clarification: "What verse suggests that to you?"

10. Discourage overuse of cross references. Learn all you can from the passage at hand, while selectively incorporating a few important references suggested in the studyguide.

11. Some questions are marked with a ✄. This indicates that further information is available in the Leader's Notes at the back of the guide.

12. For more information on getting a new Bible study group started and keeping it functioning effectively, read *You Can Start a Bible Study Group* by Gladys M. Hunt and *Pilgrims in Progress: Growing Through Groups* by Jim and Carol Plueddemann. (Both books are available from Shaw Books.)

SUGGESTIONS FOR GROUP MEMBERS

1. Learn and apply the following ground rules for effective Bible study. (If new members join the group later, review these guidelines with the whole group.)

2. Remember that your goal is to learn all you can *from the Bible passage being studied.* Let it speak for itself without using Bible commentaries or other Bible passages. There is more than enough in each assigned passage to keep your group productively occupied for one session. Sticking to the passage saves the group from insecurity ("I don't have the right reference books—or the time to read anything else.") and confusion ("Where did *that* come from? I thought we were studying _____.").

3. Avoid the temptation to bring up those fascinating tangents that don't really grow out of the passage you are discussing. If the topic is of common interest, you can bring it up later in informal conversation after the study. Meanwhile, help one another stick to the subject.

4. Encourage one another to participate. People remember best what they discover and verbalize for

themselves. Some people are naturally shy, while others may be afraid of making a mistake. If your discussion is free and friendly and you show real interest in what other group members think and feel, the quieter ones will be more likely to speak up. Remember, the more people involved in a discussion, the richer it will be.

5. Guard yourself from answering too many questions or talking too much. Give others a chance to share their ideas. If you are one who participates easily, discipline yourself by counting to ten before you open your mouth.

6. Make personal, honest applications and commit yourself to letting God's Word change you.

Introduction

Mention spiritual warfare in a Christian group and you
will get instant reactions. Some people will shy away,
feeling the topic is too controversial or frightening. Others will
jump right in, offering the newest prayer fads, book titles, or
how-to conferences. Some may go into grisly detail about the
latest satanic crimes they have heard about on a television talk
show. Still others will move to stifle the discussion, noting that
in the twentieth century we no longer need fear a primitive
vision of a man in red tights with a tail and a pitchfork.

Many of us are familiar with the term *spiritual warfare,* but
we may have trouble knowing where to get scriptural guidance
on the topic. In recent years we may have heard sermons, read
books, or listened to presentations that frankly frightened us,
and we are afraid to explore the topic because it intimidates us.
This is exactly where Satan wants us to be.

On the other hand, some of us maintain a focus on the latest findings about spiritual weapons or new prayer techniques
and formulas to use for protection against Satan. Staying too
long on this path will result in a magical approach to spiritual
warfare that sees all the problems of life as being caused by
demons and says that "right formulas" must be used to overcome demonic attacks. Though on the opposite side of the
position above, this stance, too, is exactly where Satan wants us
to be.

Is there a middle ground, and if so, where is it? A balanced
perspective on spiritual warfare is of vital importance for all

Christians because the Bible is clear that all of us are engaged in a conflict. The issue is not whether we are in the battle, but how well we are doing.

At the same time, the Bible also teaches that perspective is the key issue. We serve a sovereign God whose authority, power, love, grace, and mercy are not challenged by Satan's rebellion. Our call is to rejoice not that spirits are subject to us as Christians, but that our names are written in heaven (see Luke 10:20). Our goal is to focus on eternal issues without letting go of the realities of living on a planet under siege.

Timothy Warner, in his book *Spiritual Warfare*, writes, "The Christian life is the exciting process of trying to keep your balance." In this studyguide we will examine passages chosen to give us perspective as well as the foundational truths necessary for keeping our spiritual balance in turbulent times. My hope is that these studies will help us understand better the battle we are in and encourage us to live lives that will honor God.

In the Shadow of the Almighty

PSALM 91

How can we turn our knowledge about God
into knowledge of God? The rule for doing this
is demanding, but simple. It is that we turn
each truth that we learn about God into
matter for meditation before God,
leading to prayer and praise to God.

—J. I. PACKER, *Knowing God*

At the heart of spiritual warfare is our reliance on God's presence even in the darkest moments of life. When we feel overwhelmed by circumstances, when we are losing our grip on life, when we see no end to the tunnel or feel that we are literally walking through the valley of death, we need to be able to turn to a God who sovereignly loves us. We must have a clear and scriptural understanding of who God is and of his gracious, loving provision for us. This knowledge must penetrate down into our hearts where we can feel it and into our lives where we can see it at work.

The foundation for seeing victory in spiritual warfare is

maintaining a balanced perspective built on the actual operation of God's sovereignty in the battles we face. Such a picture is painted in Psalm 91, a psalm rich in metaphors of God's power and protection exercised on our behalf. What a wonderful place to begin this study!

1. Do you believe God is really sovereign over evil as well as over your life? Why or why not?

Read Psalm 91:1-8.

2. Four metaphors (word pictures) are used for God in verses 1 and 2. What does each of these metaphors tell you about God?

3. The psalmist used images relevant to his day. What are some images that would communicate the same ideas in contemporary terms today (e.g., God is my high-tech defense system)?

✐ 4. In verses 3, 5, and 6, the psalmist described various types of attacks. With these in mind, identify any sort of spiritual attack you may have faced recently, and discuss how you handled it.

Which one of the previous metaphors of God's provision is most meaningful for you in the circumstance you just described? Explain.

5. List the promises in verses 3-8 and briefly explain each in terms that fit contemporary life.

READ PSALM 91:9-16.

6. We are told to make God, the Most High, our dwelling (verse 9). Discuss what this might mean for you in one of the following areas of your life: your marriage, relationships with others, finances, your job, church.

What do verses 14 and 15 add to your understanding of dwelling in God?

7. Making God our dwelling is the condition for the promises that follow. How do we make God our dwelling?

8. In verses 10-13 God promises to command angels to "guard you in all your ways." How have you been aware of this sort of protection?

9. Does this promise mean that nothing bad will ever happen to Christians? Discuss.

10. Are there any limitations on the promises given in verses 14-16? Explain your answer.

11. Choose one or two promises in this psalm that you consider most significant. Explain why this promise gives you confidence when you are facing spiritual battles and struggles.

Cosmic Encounters

DANIEL 10:1–11:1; REVELATION 12:7-12

It is wrong to reject the existence of the
powers of darkness, but it is equally wrong
to believe in them in the wrong way.
—NIGEL WRIGHT, *The Satan Syndrome*

In the United States we have seen a tremendous resurgence of interest in angels and the supernatural. From television programs to best-selling books, our culture has a fascination with angels, though not necessarily the biblical variety. They are not seen as God's ministering spirits, but are often described as an advanced, nonearthly race that is looking out for humankind. Demons, if mentioned at all, are portrayed as little more than the "dark side of the force," spirits who are the equal of angels and are necessary for balancing the universe.

What is the true picture of encounters between angels and demons? Scripture affords us only a few glimpses into the domain of good and evil spirits, and the passages under consideration in this study are two of the clearest in detailing some of the events that take place out of human sight. Understanding the issues involved between good and evil spirits is another important foundation for spiritual warfare.

1. What are some of the benefits and dangers of the increased interest in angels in our culture?

READ DANIEL 10:1–11:1.

2. The nation of Israel was in captivity in Babylon when the events of this passage took place. As the passage opens, what was Daniel doing for his people (10:2)?

    Why do you think he was doing this (see Daniel 9:4-11,19-20)?

3. Daniel was not expecting an angel to appear in response to his prayer. In your own words, describe how Daniel responded when he saw the angel (10:8-9,16-17).

4. Look again at the description of this angel in 10:5-6. How would you have responded to him?

⚔ 5. Most commentators see the princes of Persia and Greece as powerful demons. What are some things we learn from this passage about Satan's strategy against God's angels (10:12-14; 10:20-11:1)?

READ REVELATION 12:7-12.

6. Who are the main characters in this final heavenly battle?

⚔ 7. *Dualism* is the concept of two equal powers opposing each other. Is this scene a picture of dualism? Explain your answer.

8. To fight successfully, we must know our enemy. What do we learn about Satan in this passage?

9. What role do Christians have in overcoming Satan (verse 11)?

✎ 10. What is your understanding of the phrase "the blood of the Lamb"?

Based upon what you see in these verses, why do you think this is an important idea for spiritual warfare?

11. What hope do you find for the ultimate victory of
good against evil in the message of verses 10-12?

12. If you feel comfortable doing so, share some of your
own "word of testimony" about Christ.

How might your testimony be used as a weapon in
the spiritual battles you face?

Know Your Enemy

ISAIAH 14:12-15; EZEKIEL 28:11-19; JOHN 8:31-49

There are two equal and opposite errors into
which our race can fall about the devils. One is
to disbelieve in their existence. The other is to
believe, and to feel an excessive and unhealthy
interest in them. They themselves are equally
pleased by both errors, and hail a materialist
or a magician with the same delight.

—C. S. LEWIS, *The Screwtape Letters*

Some people worry that by studying a topic like spiritual warfare, they are exposing themselves to danger. They reason, "If I leave Satan alone, he will leave me alone." But the assumption on which this argument is built is flawed. Satan did not leave Adam and Eve alone, he did not leave Jesus alone, and he will not leave us alone. One of his desires is to destroy our Christian walk. If we are walking as children of God, we can expect attack.

On the other side of the coin, some people act as though Satan is everywhere and knows everything. Again, this is wrong in light of biblical teachings. Satan is a limited creature, and we are called as Christians to engage in the battle against him. In this study we will explore scriptural passages that will show us more about who our enemy is.

1. When engaged in battle, why is it important to know your enemy?

READ ISAIAH 14:12-15.

ℐ 2. This passage refers to the king of Babylon (14:4), yet many feel that it also indirectly refers to Satan. Assuming this is true, what do we learn about him from this description?

3. What phrase is repeated several times?

What does this show us about what caused Satan's downfall?

ℐ 4. What was God's reaction to the desires expressed in the "I will" statements (verses 13-14)?

Do you think his response was justified? Why or why not?

5. What types of subtle "I will" statements do you sometimes live by?

READ EZEKIEL 28:11-19.

 6. This prophecy is directed against the king of Tyre (see 28:1), but it is often cited as a reference to Satan as the power behind the king. What clues do you see in the passage that would indicate that Satan may be indirectly addressed?

7. Compare this passage with Isaiah 14:12-15. What more do we learn about Satan's character here?

8. In verses 17 and 18, God outlined some specific sins he will not tolerate. What evidence of these sins do you see in our culture today?

READ JOHN 8:31-49.

9. How did Jesus define freedom?

How did the Jews define this term (verse 33)?

10. Contrast Jesus' definition of freedom with what our own society teaches us about what it means to be "free."

What are some ways in which our society is not free, but enslaved?

↗ 11. The *fatherhood of God* is a term used by many today. What ideas of fatherhood did Jesus express throughout this passage?

In light of this passage, what does it mean for us to say that God is our Father?

↗ 12. How is the devil described in verse 44?

What are some ways Satan destroys and, metaphorically, murders people?

🖉 13.   This passage gives a clear picture of people who
        thought they had the market on religious truth,
        when in reality they had fallen for Satan's lies.
        Discuss some ways we can fight our enemy Satan,
        who is by his very nature a murderer and a liar.

The Heavenly Wager

JOB 1:1–2:10

*I need to be so utterly God's, that he can
use me or hide me, as he chooses, as an
arrow in his hand or in his quiver.
I will ask no questions: I relinquish all
rights to him who desires my supreme good.*

—HELEN ROSEVEARE, *Living Sacrifice*

A cursory survey of the history of humankind will reveal
that trials are part and parcel of life itself. It is only in the
last few centuries, with the advent of industrialization and the
comforts and conveniences of modern life, that this reality has
been questioned. Why stay hot if air conditioning is available?
Why walk when cars are so easy to access? Why wash clothes
by hand when reliable washing machines will do the job for
you? Why suffer with a headache when you can take a pill? All
of these technological advances certainly alleviate many dis-
comforts, but they will never eliminate the fact that life is difficult and all of us must face trials.

Unfortunately, along with our modern appliances and conveniences has come a general attitude that we have a right to a
quick and comfortable solution to *any* problem we face. Why

work hard to write a paper for school when paper-writing services are available? Why suffer a minor injury in silence when a lawsuit may make you rich? Why stay in a painful marriage when a divorce is easy to obtain?

In light of our modern context, Job's story may at first seem old-fashioned and out of date. However, a closer look at the substance of his trials shows that his experience is timeless, and his attitude through trials continues to provide a model for us today.

1. In what areas do you struggle with wanting instant solutions to tough problems?

READ JOB 1:1-12.

2. What do you learn about Job's character from these verses?

3. Why do you think Satan was roaming the earth (verse 7)?

READ JOB 1:13–2:10.

4. What examples of Satan's power do you see here?

5. How does Satan's accusation of Job in 2:4-5 differ from his prior one in 1:9-11?

6. Note Job's reactions in 1:20-22 and 2:8-10. How do you think he was able to maintain this perspective?

7. Job attributed his trials to God (1:21). What difference might it have made if he had known about Satan's hand in them?

8. Put yourself in Job's place. Which would have been the hardest test for you to face?

🌱 9. What do Satan's responses to God in both encounters show us about Satan's character?

10. In what way was Satan on trial in this passage?

🌱 11. In what way was God on trial in this passage?

12. Job never confronted or rebuked Satan or the attacks. Instead, he kept his focus on God's continuing sovereignty and mercy. What are some practical steps you can take to maintain the same perspective as Job?

Tempting Propositions

Temptation is a factor in the psychological and
spiritual growth process everyone must go
through if we are to become mature individuals,
capable of living a full and meaningful life.
The function of temptation is always to trigger
a choice and provoke a definite stand or action.

—BOB MUMFORD, *The Purpose of Temptation*

emptation has become an almost innocuous word today, a word that is not taken too seriously. We may be "tempted" to eat some chocolate, but I doubt that the fate of the world hangs in the balance if we give in. However, it is Satan's nature to tempt us to take seemingly unimportant, small steps away from God's expressed will and down unmarked paths that can eventually lead to our destruction. This truth came to life for me shortly after my family and I returned from Africa to live in the United States.

I had accepted a one-year position and felt insecure about our future. When I became aware of a statewide lottery that was constantly being advertised, I found myself reasoning, "Wouldn't it be great if God provided for my needs that way?

Just think of how much money I could give away!" The reality is that I was feeling financially insecure, and there was definite appeal in an "instant" answer to my problem. After a period of struggle, I came to grips with the fact that placing my hopes in a lottery of any type was confusing financial security with true life security. We need to be ready at all times to recognize the all-too-gentle nudges of the Enemy that lead us away from trusting in God's established order.

1. What types of temptations—personal, financial, relational—do you face when you are feeling insecure?

READ GENESIS 3:1-13.

2. All people have needs for security and significance. How did Satan appeal to those needs in the temptation of Adam and Eve?

3. What's the difference between Eve's restatement of God's command in verse 2 and his actual command in 2:16-17?

In what ways do we add to God's commands today?

4. Why do you suppose Satan didn't simply *force* Eve to take the forbidden fruit?

5. In what ways did Satan's promise in verse 5 come true? What part did he leave out?

6. Did Satan follow any logical progression in the temptation sequence? Explain your answer.

READ LUKE 4:1-13.

7. Who wanted Jesus to face temptation (verse 1)?
Why do you think this was necessary?

8. What evidence do you find in this passage that Jesus
experienced the same physical needs and needs for
security that all human beings face?

How did Satan's temptations appeal to these needs
in Jesus?

9. What was Jesus' attitude toward Scripture? How can
we develop the same attitude?

10. Satan showed Jesus the kingdoms of the world in all their splendor, but he conveniently overlooked their sinful and destructive aspects. What does that tell us about the nature of temptation?

11. Identify the main thrusts of Jesus' temptations. In what ways does Satan use these same kinds of temptations in our lives today?

12. In light of the passages in this study, what is one practical step you can take to prepare yourself for your next encounter with temptation?

Battle Imagery

LUKE 11:14-28; 2 CORINTHIANS 10:1-6

*It need not surprise us that as an image
to convey the nature of Christian living,
the Holy Spirit uses that of warfare.
No image could be more apt.*

—JOHN WHITE, *The Fight*

The Bible portrays the Christian life as a struggle against a violent enemy. It is clear that we are engaged in a spiritual war. Perhaps our immediate response to this picture is to jump up and enter the battle, weapons blazing. Such a response may be built upon a myth I call the "joy of the fight" that is so prevalent in our culture. The image of joy found in fighting pervades our culture and is seen in a spectrum of events from children's entertainment (where the heroes beat up the villains) to sports (where the opponent must be crushed). This myth persuades us that engaging in forceful and intense fighting is the key to overcoming the enemy. It also conveys the message that violent battle somehow adds a heady spice to life, which we must drink before we are truly alive.

God's kingdom, however, is not a kingdom of violence. Jesus confronted evil firmly, but he did not ultimately overcome

Satan by beating him up. Instead, Jesus overcame Satan by loving others and submitting to God's plan of death on the cross. As Christians we are called to maintain an eternal perspective: We balance our Christian walk by studying the scriptural images of spiritual warfare and being aware of the battle, while choosing to engage in spiritual warfare as Jesus did.

1. Are you comfortable with battle and warfare imagery to describe your spiritual life? Explain.

   What are the advantages and dangers of such imagery?

READ LUKE 11:14-28.

2. Note the different responses of the people to Jesus' driving out a demon. Why do you think some people responded negatively to Jesus' ministry?

3. Of what did some people accuse Jesus (verse 15)?

4. In what terms did Jesus couch his response to their accusations (verses 17-23)?

5. What is the main point of the story in verses 21-23?

How does this story relate to or expand on Jesus' claim in verse 20?

6. What might the parable of the empty house be warning us about (verses 24-26)?

7. What do we learn about spiritual warfare priorities from Jesus' response to the woman's statement (verses 27-28)?

READ 2 CORINTHIANS 10:1-6.

8. What military imagery did the apostle Paul use to describe how Christians should relate to the world?

9. How do our weapons of spiritual warfare differ from the weapons of earthly warfare (verses 4-5)?

✎ 10. The "strongholds" Paul mentioned in verse 4 are mental patterns of thought that have become habits and can ultimately become a defense against the gospel. What are some mental strongholds you face in your own life?

✎ 11. What are some ways in which these strongholds can be overcome?

Jesus in Battle

MARK 5:1-20; 9:14-29

*Jesus came not only to deal with the problem of
sin in the world, but also to deal with God's
prime supernatural opponent—Satan himself!*

—CLINTON ARNOLD, *Powers of Darkness*

One cool, overcast afternoon I was teaching a science class
to high-school students in Swaziland, a small country in
southern Africa. Suddenly, a girl cried out, began to shake and
moan, and fell to the floor writhing. Though I suspected there
was demonic involvement, I did not know how to act on my
suspicion. I managed to calm the girl down, and we let her lie
on a couch in one of the school offices until she returned to normal. I later learned that she had in fact been the target of a form
of "love magic" practiced in Swaziland. My science training had
taught me to solve many physical problems, but it had not prepared me to deal with demonic power when I encountered it.

There are several accounts in the Gospels in which Jesus
faced demons. Jesus knew the demonic from the physical, and
he knew what to do when confronted directly with the powers
of evil. In today's study we will see three components of spiritual
warfare: Jesus' power over demons, his frustration with the

disciples' inability to minister effectively, and his compassion toward those facing the reality of the demonic in their own lives.

1. Why do you think people are so fascinated with the occult and the supernatural?

READ MARK 5:1-20.

∂ 2. One aspect of being human is bearing God's image (see Genesis 1:27). In light of this truth, in what ways were the demonized man's actions inhuman (verses 2-5)?

∂ 3. What do you see as the main characteristics and goals of the demons based on verses 1-13?

What were the evil spirits afraid of in this confrontation with Jesus (verses 7,10-12)?

∂ 4. Did the spirits come out at Jesus' first command?

What lesson or clues for spiritual confrontation might this fact provide?

5. Why did Jesus not permit the man to accompany him (verses 18-20)?

6. The man in this account never actually professed faith in Christ. What evidence is there of his belief?

READ MARK 9:14-29.

7. What symptoms of demonic control do you see in this passage?

8. Whom was Jesus addressing in verse 19?

Why was he so frustrated with them?

9. Why do you think Jesus took the time to question the father rather than immediately rebuking the demon?

10. Why did the disciples fail (verses 18-19,23,28-29)?

What can we learn from their failure?

11. Some say that demons are not real and that Jesus was simply accommodating himself to the people and culture of his time. How would you respond to this idea?

12. Which of the main characters do you relate to more: the father or the disciples? Why?

13. Summarize in a sentence or two what you see as the most important lesson for your life from these two stories.

The Church in Battle

Acts 16:11-34; 19:8-20

In God's topsy-turvy approach to power, he takes
weak, scarred, scared, struggling, failing and
ineffective people and accomplishes his mighty
work with such miserably inadequate tools.

—Richard Girard, *My Weakness: His Strength*

It can be exhilarating to see demons submit to Christ's authority. The experience can leave us with a heady mixture of power and the feeling that God is using us in a significant way. There is a subtle temptation in such exhilaration, however. Too much focus on our authority and power in Christ can lead us toward a "power trip" that can be deadly. Great care must be taken to ensure that our delight in the exercise of spiritual authority does not replace our delight in Christ as our Savior.

All of us would agree that balance in spiritual warfare is critical. At the same time, few of us can ever admit that we may be out of balance and in need of correction. How can we ensure the maintenance of balance in this area? Observing how the apostle Paul dealt with these issues can help us toward that end.

1. Why do you think it is so easy to lose balance and
    go to extremes in spiritual warfare?

READ ACTS 16:11-34.

🌿 2. Paul encountered several people in Philippi. Briefly
       describe how the gospel affected each of the following:

Lydia (verses 11-15)

the slave girl (verses 16-18)

the slave girl's owners (verses 19-21)

the city magistrates (verses 22-24)

the jailer (verses 29-34)

🌿 3. How is evangelism—sharing the good news of
       Christ with others—one of our most aggressive acts
       of spiritual warfare?

4. How did Paul respond to the demonized girl (verses 17-18)?

5. The demonized girl was set free, but her owners were unhappy. What do you see of Satan's counter-attacks in this incident?

6. How did Paul and Silas respond to Satan's attack?

7. Do you think their imprisonment and persecution meant spiritual defeat? Why or why not?

READ ACTS 19:8-12.

8. What roles did teaching and miracles play in Paul's ministry and in spiritual warfare at Ephesus?

9. Do you think the way God worked in this instance (verses 11-12) can be used as a ministry method today? Explain your answer.

What might be the dangers of basing ministry on accounts such as this one?

READ ACTS 19:13-20.

10. Why did the exorcists fail in their experimental use of Jesus' name?

11. The Christians responded to this event by destroying their magical paraphernalia. Why is this kind of response a significant part of spiritual warfare?

12. In both of these accounts, what was the ultimate result of Spirit-led spiritual warfare?

13. What can we learn from these passages about keeping a balance between good and bad uses of authority and power?

Seated with a Purpose

EPHESIANS 1:15–2:10

You don't have to outshout him or outmuscle him to be free of his influence. You just have to outtruth him. Believe, declare, and act upon the truth of God's Word, and you will thwart Satan's strategy.

—NEIL ANDERSON, *The Bondage Breaker*

M any people have a picture of spiritual warfare that is filled with exotic and frightening battles with demons. Certainly we see such encounters in the gospel accounts that show powerful evidence of Jesus' work in disarming Satan. But is that the only image of spiritual conflict portrayed in Scripture? It helps to realize that demons or evil spirits are mentioned only five times in the entire book of Acts, which covers some thirty years of the early church's history. There are no rituals or exact formulas to be followed, nor are there exhortations to establish ministries that deal explicitly with demonized people. Paul's epistles also omit any explicit instructions regarding demonic encounters. Rather than finding methodologies for contests of power, we see a focus on truth as a foundation for spiritual warfare, truth that is to be known and lived out in real-life settings.

In the book of Ephesians, Paul sets forth what might be

called a bird's-eye perspective on the Christian life. He presents to us what we should know about God, what we were and what we have now become, and how that fits into God's design in calling us to Christ. Paul lays the doctrinal foundation necessary for us to see how spiritual warfare fits into the larger context of Christian living.

1. How do you think spiritual warfare fits into the whole of the Christian life?

READ EPHESIANS 1:15-23.

2. What three things did Paul pray that the believers in Ephesus would *know* (verses 18-19)?

3. Why is knowing each of these things important for us as Christians?

4. What is the scope and effect of Christ's position (verses 20-21)?

What are the implications of this fact for spiritual warfare?

5. How did Paul describe unbelievers (verse 1)?

Do you think most non-Christians see themselves this way? Explain your answer.

6. Paul used several terms for Satan in verse 2. What clues do these give us about Satan's character and authority?

⚭ 7. Identify the three ways Paul observed that unbelievers are influenced by evil (verses 2-3).

Discuss some ways each of these areas can lead us away from Christ.

8. In contrast to what we were, what have we become as a result of God's power working on our behalf (verses 5-6,10)?

9. Why has God "seated us with [Christ] in the heavenly realms" (verses 6)?

What do you think this spiritual reality means?

🖉 10. What are some of the implications for spiritual warfare of *our* being seated *with* Christ (verses 5-10)?

🖉 11. Summarize the main points of Ephesians 1:15–2:10.
Find one application for your own life right now
and share it with the group.

Battle Armor

EPHESIANS 6:10-18; 1 PETER 5:6-11

*Some Christians are so self-confident that they think
they can manage by themselves without the Lord's
strength and armour. Others are so self-distrustful that
they imagine they have nothing to contribute to their
victory in spiritual warfare. Both are mistaken.*

—JOHN STOTT, *God's New Society*

Soldiers who go into battle without weapons are foolish,
and they are often wounded or killed before they have
the chance to understand the consequences of their foolish-
ness. Christians are just as foolish if we do not make use of the
weapons God has provided for us when we face Satan's attacks.

Just as important as *having* these weapons, however, is
knowing how and when to use them. The weapons God has
given are not to be fired occasionally and then stored for future
need. Rather, they involve daily, disciplined use lest we be overcome by the tricks and traps of the Enemy.

1. How can ignorance of our spiritual weaponry hurt
   us as Christians?

READ EPHESIANS 6:10-18.

2. How are we to be strong in the Lord (verses 10,13)?

3. How does Paul describe our spiritual battle (verses 11-12)?

How have you experienced this reality in your own life?

4. What are some implications of the fact that many of our struggles are not against flesh and blood?

Does Paul's statement mean that Satan is behind *everything* bad that happens to us? Discuss.

5. Identify the spiritual weapons we have at our disposal.

6. Explain how you think each weapon can be used by Christians to enable them to stand against Satan's attacks.

7. How does prayer hold all of these together?

8. What does Paul tell us to pray about (verse 18)?

How does this relate to spiritual warfare?

READ I PETER 5:6-11.

9. Peter tells us to humble ourselves before God. Why is this so difficult for people to do?

10. What are some ways we can resist Satan (verses 6-9)?

11. What is one area of your life in which you need to discipline yourself (verse 8)?

12. What do we learn about God in verses 10 and 11?

Which aspect of these verses is most meaningful to you right now? Why?

Battle Tactic: Freedom Through Forgiving

MATTHEW 18:21-35; 1 CORINTHIANS 5:1-5;
2 CORINTHIANS 2:5-11

*A Christian will find it cheaper to pardon than
to resent. Forgiveness saves the expense of anger,
the cost of hatred, the waste of spirits.*

—HANNAH MORE

The young man in my office had staked out his claim. He was going home to confront his father and see who was really in control of the house. I probed gently, seeing deep pain embedded in their relationship. I decided to come at it directly and asked him, "Have you ever considered forgiving your father?"

"No, and I don't want to," he curtly replied.

In a sense I knew that his spiritual struggle would not be finished until he was able to honestly face and release the anger and hurt that had become his comfortable companions.

Forgiving those who have hurt us is a topic that is often neglected in churches today. We live in a revenge-dominated society that would rather settle things through a lawsuit than through Christian forgiveness, and Satan wants to keep us divided. Yet who of us has not experienced the exuberant joy and freedom when we have been forgiven and a relationship has been made right? Forgiveness needs to be restored to its rightful place as one of the most important and powerful spiritual weapons in the Christian's arsenal.

1. What do you think it means to forgive someone who has hurt you?

READ MATTHEW 18:21-35.

2. Peter was possibly expecting praise for his generous attitude, since to forgive someone seven times would have been exceeding the religious requirements of the day (verse 21). What was the gist of Jesus' response to Peter's question?

How do you think Peter may have felt as he listened to Jesus' story?

3. What steps did the master take to forgive the huge debt the servant owed?

4. What kept the ungrateful servant from forgiving the man who owed him one hundred denarii?

5. A popular idea in our churches today is that forgiveness means forgetting. In this story, however, the master did not forget the debt—he even resurrected it! Is this true forgiveness? Discuss.

6. How does our vertical relationship with God relate to our horizontal relationships with others (verses 32-33)?

7. Think of a time when you acted like the ungrateful servant or when someone acted that way toward you. How did you feel? How did you deal with it?

8. Why is it so important for us to forgive those who "owe" us?

Should there be any limitations on our forgiveness of others? Explain.

READ 1 CORINTHIANS 5:1-5 AND 2 CORINTHIANS 2:5-11.

9. Forgiveness affects us not only personally but also corporately. How did church discipline and forgiveness work together in this situation in the Corinthian church?

10. What was the basis of Paul's call to the Corinthians to forgive the man in this incident (2 Corinthians 2:6-7)?

11. A spirit of unforgiveness often comes from our own weaknesses. What more did Paul recognize as being part of the church's struggle in this situation (2 Corinthians 2:11)?

12. What are some advantages Satan gains when Christians do not forgive each other?

In what ways might this apply to you right now?

Battle Attitude: Loving Boldly

ROMANS 12

*Bold love is courageously setting aside our personal
agenda to move humbly into the world of others
with their well-being in view, willing to risk further
pain in our souls, in order to be an aroma of life to
some and an aroma of death to others.*

—DAN ALLENDER AND TREMPER LONGMAN III, *Bold Love*

It often seems that the church is back on its heels in a
purely defensive stance against Satan's attacks. But we are
also called to take aggressive, positive steps in this spiritual
battle. By taking the offensive, we must guard against the
danger of becoming like the enemy we are fighting—hateful
and vengeful. We must not lose track of God's call to live and
love as Jesus did.

What does it mean to love those who hate us and attack
us? How can we seek their good while they are seeking to
destroy us? The ability to love and bless our enemies can only
come from the unshakable realization of who we are in Christ
and of God's overruling sovereignty in the daily affairs of life.

This is the crux of spiritual warfare on the practical level. Love disarms the power of hate and is our most potent weapon against evil.

1. Christians are to love one another. What are some creative ways in which you have loved others or have been shown love in difficult situations?

READ ROMANS 12:1-8.

2. Paul challenges us to find appropriate ways to thank God for his mercy shown to us through Christ. With this in mind, what does it mean on a practical, daily level to offer our bodies as "living sacrifices, holy and pleasing to God" (verse 1)?

3. Why is it so important for us to think of ourselves with "sober judgment" as we relate to others (verse 3)?

4. How can the gifts mentioned in verses 6-8 be used
   to love others boldly?

5. We know that Satan is a liar and a murderer. In
   light of this fact, what are some ways he might
   tempt us to abuse spiritual gifts in our churches?

READ ROMANS 12:9-21.

6. How did Paul say we are to overcome evil (verses
   9,21)?

   What practical ways did he offer for doing this
   (verses 10-20)?

7. In what ways can love be insincere?

8. Read carefully each command found in verses 9-13. Choose one command and tell how it might be used in spiritual warfare to thwart and overcome evil in the church.

9. Bold love demands that we bless those who persecute us (verse 14). What does this mean?

What attitudes are necessary for us to obey this command wholeheartedly?

10. What are some of the ways Satan uses the desire for revenge to gain an advantage over people and to divide Christians?

11. Paul encourages us to live at peace with one another (verse 18). Is there a difficult situation you face in which a peaceful solution depends on you? How can you deal with that situation in a loving way?

12. In light of the many ideas in this passage, discuss some positive steps you will take to begin to love more boldly. Be specific.

13. How have the lessons in this studyguide expanded your understanding of the different aspects of spiritual warfare?

Which study has been the most meaningful? Why?

Leader's Notes

STUDY 1: IN THE SHADOW OF THE ALMIGHTY

Question 2. Each metaphor in Psalm 91:1-2 is associated with a different name of God and a basic idea: *Shelter*—God the *Most High* (who shields us from attack); *Shadow*—God the *Almighty* (the One who stands over us for safety); *Refuge*—God the LORD (we can go to him for sanctuary); *Fortress*—God *my God* (he is not just God, but *my* God).

"This is a psalm for danger: for times of exposure and encirclement or of challenging the power of evil" (Derek Kidner, *Psalms 73–150*, Downers Grove, IL: InterVarsity, 1975, p. 331). The basic thrust is that we can have confidence in God's protection and security during times of vulnerability. This is the foundation for spiritual warfare.

Question 4. A *fowler* (Psalm 91:3) is one who traps birds (see Jeremiah 5:26). Some commentators feel the images in verses 3, 5, and 6 refer to demons, but it is more likely that these images are intended simply as metaphors for physical and spiritual attacks in which our trust in God is tested.

Question 6. Jesus later talked about our "remaining" in him (see John 15:1-10). This passage may provide help in thinking through the implications of making God our dwelling.

Question 8. The promise is one of the ministries of angels who are sent to serve Christians (see Hebrews 1:14). However, they are sent at God's request, not at our demand. Satan tried to get

Jesus to abuse this promise by turning it into a frivolous test (see Matthew 4:6-7). Jesus responded by noting that the issue is not testing, but trusting.

Question 10. Some Christians take these promises so literally that they encourage people to "prove" their faith by forcing God's hand. Though God delights in meeting our needs, he will never be under our control. That would be contrary to his nature as the Sovereign One. We rest in his promise of protection, but we are not to test him just to assure ourselves that he is really there.

STUDY 2: COSMIC ENCOUNTERS

Question 2. Daniel was praying, but more specifically he was repenting on behalf of the exiles.

Question 5. If nothing else, we do see that Satan divides responsibilities among demons and that he seeks to influence countries at the highest level through them.

Question 7. An example of dualism is seen in the good and dark sides of the "force" in the Star Wars movies. With true dualism, you never really know which side will win, since each side has equal powers and capabilities.

Question 10. The "blood of the Lamb" is often misused as a type of magic formula that protects us when we utter it. The term is a symbol of the reality of Christ's death, and our use of it implies our willing surrender to the significance of Christ's death on our behalf. As one writer states, the blood of the

Lamb "is not a kind of magic charm, a ritual that we import into sermon or prayer to attest to our orthodoxy or to secure supernatural results. It is not a formula to be credulously mumbled, nor is it a parroting of mystical words. It is the expression of an intelligent, active, vital faith in Christ, the Lamb of God, who, by the shedding of his blood, bruised Satan's head and utterly defeated him.... So then, when in prayer we plead the blood of the Lamb, we are really saying that our faith is resting for victory over Satan and sin upon all that Christ achieved for us by his victorious death and victorious resurrection" (J. Oswald Sanders, *Satan Is No Myth*, Chicago: Moody Press, 1975, pp. 121-122).

Question 12. As the term is used here, my *testimony* is more than just the story of how I came to faith; it is also my verbal declaration of the truth of God as revealed by Jesus and as it works in my life.

STUDY 3: KNOW YOUR ENEMY

Question 2. Bible scholars are divided as to whether Satan is indirectly addressed here. The exaggerated language is seen as an important clue. In Isaiah 14:12, the term *morning star* is literally "Lucifer." This verse is the source for our use of *Lucifer* as one of the names for Satan. The issues of his character are seen in the "I will" statements in verses 13 and 14.

Question 4. God's response is based on the simple fact that he is the Creator and sustainer of all things. God does not demand our submission; he simply deserves it as the One who made us. He will not brook attempts by any of the created order to impose our will over his, for to do so would be to deny his sovereign nature. In modern terms, he is the inventor of creation, he owns the "patent" on it, and he deserves the "royalties." Our humble submission to him is simply the expression that we recognize his place and ours in the universe.

Question 6. Evangelical Bible commentators are divided as to whether this passage applies to Satan. As with the Isaiah passage, the most important factor used by those in favor of applying this description to Satan is the exaggerated language found in Ezekiel 28:12-16.

Question 10. The freedom Jesus brings is the freedom from sin, and thus the freedom to obey God. In our day and age, we tend to view freedom as the right to do whatever we want to do, whenever and however we want to do it. For example, many in our culture demand the freedom of alternate sexual lifestyles, not realizing the slavery into which they are falling. Others want to be free from all authority, while living out the lives of slavery to rebellion. Still others demand that we keep our morals to ourselves and live as captives to their physical desires.

Question 11. Fatherhood is not limited to physical descent or legal adoption. The central issue here is that of the children showing the character of their true father.

Question 12. In John 8:44 the word *murderer* is used literally. As a metaphor, it can indicate the destruction of people as human beings as well as the dissolution of our relationships with other people.

In the Garden of Eden, God promised Adam and Eve that

they would die if they disobeyed. Though they did not physically die at the moment of their disobedience, they set into action a chain of events that ultimately led to their physical deaths. The immediate death they experienced was spiritual and emotional. This is seen in the "death" of their relationships with God (they hid from God) and with each other (they had to cover themselves). Satan, the tempter who set the whole sequence into motion, in effect murdered Adam and Eve. Jesus indicates this with the words "he was a murderer from the beginning" (verse 44).

Question 13. Have the group focus on issues related to preservation or restoration (e.g., in relationships) and various means of using the truth to show a lie for what it is. Help the group think through personal applications such as taking steps to restore a broken relationship or memorizing scripture so as to have access to the truth in their hearts.

STUDY 4: THE HEAVENLY WAGER

Question 3. The picture of Satan "roaming" does not have to be a literal one, though the possibility of his literally roaming around cannot be discounted. First Peter 5:8 indicates a roughly similar idea, but the purpose is clearly delineated. However he does it as a spirit being, Satan is on the lookout for possible victims and intends to pounce when he finds them.

Question 9. Satan is an accuser who cannot believe in the integrity of any person. His arrogance is seen in that even when he is proven wrong by God himself, he does not repent! He defies and contradicts God at every opportunity.

Question 11. Perhaps one reason God allows testing is to show evil for what it is. His actions are fully justified, and he desires that we understand this truth and trust him.

STUDY 5: TEMPTING PROPOSITIONS

Question 3. The reason for Eve's addition of not touching the fruit is debated by scholars. It may simply be zeal, or it may be that Adam passed the command on to Eve in this form. Before we self-righteously condemn Adam or Eve for this addition, we should at least note that it does show a desire to obey God. Unfortunately, the adding of human requirements to God's law was not limited to the garden—we still do it all too often today in various forms of legalism. Some, for example, require or prohibit certain types of dress. Others focus on behaviors such as dancing or drinking. Still others add spiritual requirements (devotions, religious service or ministry, works, etc.). While God has created and saved us for good works, these works are not the means of our salvation (see Ephesians 2:8-10).

Question 4. If Eve had been forced to take the fruit, she could have rightly claimed to be a victim. As it turned out, she still placed the blame on Satan (Genesis 3:13), but God did not accept her excuse. Satan's desire was to lead Adam and Eve down the path of rebellion against God, and to do this successfully, he had to convince her rather than coerce her.

Question 6. One way a progression moves is from questioning God's command (Genesis 3:1) to questioning and contradicting his word and his ability to carry out his promise (verses 4-

5) to finally rejecting him. Due to the brevity of this narrative, we see nothing more than a broad progression.

Question 8. In the Incarnation, Jesus became fully human. He experienced all the same human needs and desires as we do, and yet he did not sin when confronting the reality of those needs. In fact, because he never sinned, we may justifiably conclude that he faced the reality of these needs *more* than we ever do, since we tend to give in all too quickly to inappropriate means of fulfilling our needs.

Question 9. The Old Testament had not only been part of Jesus' education but also part of his very lifestyle. He had Scripture passages memorized, though not like a student ready for a pop quiz. His responding to temptation with appropriate scriptures came from his intimacy with God's Word rather than just a superficial memorization program.

STUDY 6: BATTLE IMAGERY

Question 3. While commentators are unsure of the derivation of the term *Beelzebub,* they are all agreed that it refers to Satan. In Matthew's account of this event (12:24), we read that it was the Pharisees who made this accusation against Jesus. The Pharisees were religious leaders who stressed individual fulfillment of Jewish law as the means of religious righteousness. They were threatened by Jesus' popular actions and teaching, and so they had to find some way to discredit him. The context of his response is this ongoing debate and not purely a question of whether he used satanic power to fight against Satan.

One commentator has observed that this accusation does not refer to Satan's own deceptive tactics by which demons are supposedly "cast out" through magical practices. Such "exorcisms" are little more than "keen Satanic strategy and diabolic miracle to build up and spread out the empire of evil" (Merrill Unger, *Biblical Demonology*, Wheaton, IL: Scripture Press, 1963, pp. 103-104). They are more likely examples of Satan shifting his forces through deception than of Satan genuinely expelling his own demons.

Question 6. "The point of the story is not to give interesting facts about demonic ecology but to warn against the fearful danger of a repentance that is purely negative. A relapse can lead to dreadful danger.... Opinions differ as to whether this story is meant to be taken literally or as a parable of spiritual deterioration" (*New Bible Commentary*, rev. ed., Grand Rapids: Eerdmans, 1970, p. 906). We might add that even if it is only a warning about "spiritual deterioration," Satan's goals are still being accomplished.

Question 7. You might also have the group read Luke 10:17-20. In this account the disciples return from their travels, flushed with success and delighted that demons submitted to them in Jesus' name. Jesus reminded them that it is more important that their names are in the Book of Life than that demons submitted to them. One ever-present danger for those ministering in the area of demonic confrontation is the loss of perspective.

Question 10. We are not computers, but we do respond to programming that has been burned into us by those around us and by our environment. Typically, demonic strongholds are built on false ideas about God or self. These false ideas are most visibly expressed in un-Christlike temperaments and behavior patterns of which an unlimited number may be found in our culture. For example, children from abusive families struggle to see God as Father in the best sense of the word. We also have nonbiblical proverbs, such as "Don't get mad, get even," and "God helps those who help themselves," which many quote and follow as a lifestyle.

Question 11. Paul mentioned that we are to take our thoughts captive and make them obedient to Christ. This does not refer to every stray thought that comes our way; that would be parallel to confessing every temptation as sin. But when evil thoughts come, we must refuse to give them "free air time" by dismissing them for what they are. This is similar to our refusal to give room for temptation to entice us to sin. When we find ourselves dwelling on false ideas about God or ourselves (e.g., "God is absent" or "I am worthless"), then we can consciously take them captive and bring them to the throne of Christ. One of the best ways to do this is to appropriate the scripture you have memorized to facilitate a biblical response to the mental stronghold.

STUDY 7: JESUS IN BATTLE

Question 2. Help the group see the many ways in the passage in which the demons are defacing human dignity in their victim.

Question 3. Look at Luke 8:26-29 for additional details that may help highlight demonic intentions and character.

Question 4. Mark 5:8 and Luke 8:29 indicate that Jesus had commanded the demons to come out, but they had not yet done so. This serves as a reminder that Jesus is dealing with rebellious living beings, not blindly devoted robots.

Question 7. Several symptoms of demonic activity are found in the passage. It is important to keep in mind that any single symptom in and of itself is not always proof of demonization; the full picture must be kept in mind.

Question 8. This "unbelieving generation" refers to the disciples. Keep the context of Mark 9:2-13 in mind. Jesus had come down from his transfiguration only to see his disciples, who had previously cast out demons, now embarrassed and unsuccessful in helping the man.

Question 11. One type of response might be as follows: If demons were not real, it makes sense to think that Jesus would have then used these times to teach that they did not exist. Instead, he implied they were real by casting them out.

Study 8: The Church in Battle

Question 2. This chapter begins in the middle of the second of Paul's three missionary journeys. He had just finished working his way from Asia Minor (modern Turkey) to Macedonia (modern Greece). The city of Philippi, which was Paul's first major stop, was a Roman colony in the province of Macedonia. Because Paul went to the place of prayer first, we know there was probably not a synagogue or many Jews in the city. The fruit of this first visit was the planting of a new church.

Lydia quietly turned to Christ and was, incidentally, the first convert from Paul's ministry in Europe.

The slave girl was possessed by a spirit (literally a "pythonic spirit") whom her owners believed to be Apollo, the Greek god associated with fortune telling. To put this incident in perspective, we must remember that this type of spectacular spiritual warfare encounter is seen rarely in Acts (demons or evil spirits are mentioned only five times in the book). Luke's general emphasis was on the expansion of the church, and direct encounters with demons form only occasional elements of the total story.

Question 3. Jesus came to set the captives free from sin as well as evil, and they are set free primarily through believing in Jesus' death and resurrection.

Question 4. She had been following them for days, and it is easy to imagine Paul growing tired of the free advertising she was giving them with her shouting. He used no ritual, and his claim on Christ's name was based on his understanding of the authority of the Christian, not on a special formula to affect the expulsion. Keep the group responses focused not on the power or the apostolic authority, but on the simplicity of the encounter.

Question 6. Bear in mind that Paul and Silas had been beaten severely before being put into jail. Additionally, they were put into stocks and secured in the innermost part of the prison. It is likely that they were isolated from the rest of the prisoners and had to sing loudly before they could be heard. The attitude of Paul and Silas is critical. Even when Satan had apparently won a skirmish, they continued to trust God. They were obviously ready to face persecution that rose from their preaching of the gospel and did not consider that persecution as spiritual defeat. God honored their faith and also his promise to use Paul to reach the Gentiles for Christ. This is seen both in their release and their continued freedom to preach the gospel as well as in the conversion of the jailer. Paul and Silas took Satan's attack of imprisonment and turned it into an opportunity to proclaim the release of the captives!

Question 8. This was Paul's second visit to Ephesus. The first time was on his second missionary journey (Acts 18:18-21). This time he stayed in Ephesus for more than two years. Ephesus was one of the greatest commercial cities in Asia Minor (modern Turkey). It was a harbor city on the main trade route from Rome to the East. Spiritually speaking, it was a city known for its magical practitioners and their abilities to cure. This is perhaps the reason for God's working of extraordinary miracles through Paul here.

Question 9. The book of Acts is a descriptive account of the events in the growth of the early church. The handkerchief miracles were a one-time event, which the author Luke describes. If this were a type of ministry God wanted to initiate, we would expect to see it either reproduced elsewhere in the New Testament or at least discussed as a form of ministry in one of the Epistles. If people hope to reproduce this type of ministry, then they should not tie it to "donations" as a medium of exchange for blessed handkerchiefs. That would be nothing more than luring people to buy God's blessings, which are not for sale at any price.

Question 11. This passage should be kept in context and not be used to advocate public book burning. First, the Christians voluntarily burned their own books, not books that belonged to a public institution. Second, they were not burning normal literature, but magical scrolls that were used as "cookbooks" for occultic practices. Many contained the names of demons who were to be called on for power. Third, this was a response generated by the Holy Spirit. We do not see Paul or any other leaders whipping the people into a book-burning frenzy. Rather, we see those who were practitioners of magical arts declaring publicly that they were renouncing such practices and their continued participation in them.

STUDY 9: SEATED WITH A PURPOSE

Question 2. In Ephesians 1:12-14 Paul described more about "the hope to which he has called you" and "the riches of [God's] glorious inheritance" (verse 18) we have received in 1:3-8. The implications of God's power on our behalf are described in 1:19-23. It may be helpful for the group to read these sections to identify these things before discussing why they are so important.

Question 4. In Paul's day, being seated at the ruler's right hand demonstrated that you were highly favored and shared in his authority. Paul connected this to Christ's authority over the powers known to the Ephesians, who lived in a city that was well-known for its powerful demonic magic.

Question 7. Paul pointed out that we used to follow (1) the ways of the world, (2) the ways of "the ruler of the kingdom of the air" (Satan), and (3) the ways of our own sinful thoughts and desires. More popularly we categorize these areas as the world, the flesh, and the devil. The term *world* refers to the ungodly systems that dominate our lives and try to squeeze us into blind conformity. Not limited to any particular institution, worldly systems confront us at every turn in life, such as in television (both programs and commercials), music, sports, the competitive drive, business, the focus on money and greed, and the trivialization of God in everyday American life.

Question 10. If necessary, remind the group of the previous discussion of Christ being seated above all other powers at God's right hand (Ephesians 1:20-21). Since Christ is far above all other powers, by virtue of our spiritual position with him, we, too, have access to his authority and his power over evil.

Question 11. One way of summarizing might be: We who were dead in our sins (Ephesians 2:1-3) have been saved by grace through faith (2:8-9), made alive in Christ (2:4-5), seated with him (2:6), and delegated with his matchless authority (1:18-23; 2:6), in order that we might do the good works God prepared in advance for us to do (2:10).

Study 10: Battle Armor

Question 3. Paul expanded on the idea of battling against spiritual powers by listing demonic forces in the latter half of Ephesians 6:12. This is not intended to be a catalog or a specific ranking of demons. Rather, it is simply a reminder that Satan's hosts are arrayed against the Christian, and these are the ones we are to stand against.

Question 4. Beware of the group going too far in answering this question. Paul's statement does not mean that Satan is the source behind every bad thing that happens. The opposite of seeing demons everywhere is seeing them nowhere, and both extremes are wrong.

Paul's intention is to keep us from paying too much attention to the physical and material, flesh-and-blood struggles of life to the exclusion of supernatural aspects, but he does not want us to think that every difficulty is demonic.

Question 6. Truth: We are to be people of integrity who are trustworthy before both God and others. Sins against the truth, such as unfaithfulness, expose us to Satan's attacks and remove any grounds we have for resistance. *Righteousness:* We are declared righteous in Christ and are to live in a way that reflects the truth of God's declaration about us. Living unrighteously removes us from fellowship with God and exposes us to Satan's accusations. *Gospel of peace:* We are people who have inner peace with God through faith in the gospel. As a result, we strive for outer peace with the people around us. Lack of peace is an obvious entry point for Satan's assaults. *Faith:* Faith here is not just the idea of the Christian faith; it includes our ability to trust in God's sovereign mercy in every circumstance of life. Lack of faith (doubt or unbelief) makes us easy targets for Satan's flaming darts. *Salvation:* "We are protected when we confidently rest in the fact that we are now saved and that Satan cannot remove our salvation. We are further protected as we rely on the hope of our future salvation (end times), knowing, no matter how bad the present circumstances are, that the final victory over the enemy is already secured" (A. Scott Moreau, *The World of the Spirits,* Nairobi, Kenya: Evangel Publishing House, 1990, p. 56-57).

Word of God: The Word of God refers to the appropriate use of the Bible when attacks come. The best illustration of this is Jesus' response to Satan in the temptations (see study 5). When we do not know the Word of God and how to use it, we are left defenseless against the lies of the Enemy.

Question 10. Humbling ourselves before God should not be overlooked as a spiritual weapon. It reminds us that our power and hope are only in God. Resisting Satan is found not only in standing firm in faith and facing his attacks but in going on the spiritual offensive and living humble, Christlike lives before others.

STUDY 11: BATTLE TACTIC: FREEDOM THROUGH FORGIVING

Question 3. The servant's debt of ten thousand talents was equal to millions of dollars.

Question 4. The debt of a hundred denarii was equal to a few dollars.

Question 5. The idea that forgiveness really means forgetting is not in Scripture. Though God separates us from our sins as far as the east is from the west, he is still omniscient and does not literally forget what we have done. Rather, the picture in this parable is that of removing the debt accrued to us as a result of our sin, a form of wiping clean the balance owed on the ledger without denying the existence of the sins and debt. In other words, the debt from the offenses has been released, but the reality of the offenses is not wiped out.

Question 8. Two excellent resources on the topic of personal forgiveness include *Forgiving Our Parents, Forgiving Ourselves* by David Stoop and James Masteller and *Bold Love* by Dan Allender and Tremper Longman III. Both titles are included in the list of resources and should be available through your local Christian bookstore.

Question 9. Most Bible commentators believe the same man is being discussed in these two passages. The man had been sleeping with his father's wife (probably his stepmother). Paul had commanded the Corinthian church to discipline him by expelling the man from their fellowship until he repented.

STUDY 12: BATTLE ATTITUDE: LOVING BOLDLY

Question 2. The word *therefore* in Romans 12:1 indicates that this chapter is built on what Paul said in the previous chapter. His basic thrust is that we are to offer ourselves to God not to earn righteousness before God, but as our way of thanking God for all he has done for us in Christ. In his call for us to offer our "bodies" in thanksgiving to God, Paul meant for us to offer *all* that we are in the concrete realities of life.

Question 9. Blessing others is certainly the opposite of what we want to do when we are being persecuted. At the same time, however, it will be helpful to realize that the ultimate blessing God can give to a human being is to draw that person to the foot of the cross in humble repentance. In that sense, by praying for the salvation of those who are enemies of the church, we are praying for God's blessing on them.

References and Resources

Allender, Dan and Tremper Longman III. *Bold Love.*
Colorado Springs: NavPress, 1992.

Anderson, Neil. *The Bondage Breaker.* Eugene, OR: Harvest
House, 1990.

Arnold, Clinton E. *Powers of Darkness: Principalities and Powers
in Paul's Letters.* Downers Grove, IL: InterVarsity, 1992.

Foster, Richard. *Celebration of Discipline: The Path to
Spiritual Growth.* New York: Harper & Row, 1978.

Girard, Richard. *My Weakness: His Strength.* Grand Rapids:
Zondervan, 1981.

Kidner, Derek. *Psalms 73–150.* Downers Grove, IL: InterVarsity, 1975.

Lewis, C. S. *The Screwtape Letters.* New York: Macmillan,
1961.

Moreau, A. Scott. *The World of the Spirits: A Biblical Study in
the African Context.* Nairobi, Kenya: Evangel Publishing
House, 1990.

Mumford, Bob. *The Purpose of Temptation.* New York: Revell,
1973.

Packer, J. I. *Knowing God.* Downers Grove, IL: InterVarsity,
1973.

Roseveare, Helen. *Living Sacrifice.* London: Hodder and
Stoughton, 1979.

Sanders, J. Oswald. *Satan Is No Myth.* Chicago: Moody Press,
1975.

Stoop, David and James Masteller. *Forgiving Our Parents,
Forgiving Ourselves: Healing Adult Children of Dysfunc-
tional Families.* Ann Arbor, MI: Vine Books, 1991.

Stott, John. *God's New Society. The Message of Ephesians.* Downers Grove, IL: InterVarsity, 1979.

Unger, Merrill. *Biblical Demonology.* Wheaton, IL: Scripture Press, 1963.

Warner, Timothy. *Spiritual Warfare: Victory over the Powers of This Dark World.* Wheaton, IL: Crossway, 1991.

White, John. *The Fight.* Downers Grove, IL: InterVarsity, 1979.

Wright, Nigel. *The Satan Syndrome: Putting the Power of Darkness in Its Place.* Grand Rapids: Zondervan, 1990.

The Fisherman Bible Studyguide Series—
Get Hooked on Studying God's Word

Old Testament Studies

Genesis

Proverbs

New Testament Studies

Mark

John

Acts 1-12

Acts 13-28

Romans

Philippians

Colossians

James

1, 2, 3 John

Revelation

Women of the Word

Becoming Women
of Purpose

Wisdom for
Today's Woman

Women Like Us

Women Who
Believed God

For more information, visit our Web site: www.waterbrookmultnomah.com

Topical Studies

Building Your House on the Lord

Discipleship

Encouraging Others

The Fruit of the Spirit

Growing Through Life's Challenges

Guidance and God's Will

Higher Ground

Lifestyle Priorities

The Parables of Jesus

Parenting with Purpose and Grace

Prayer

Proverbs & Parables

The Sermon on the Mount

Speaking Wisely

Spiritual Disciplines

Spiritual Gifts

Spiritual Warfare

The Ten Commandments

When Faith Is All You Have

Who Is the Holy Spirit?